Get Out of Your Own Way:

A Guide to Confidence & Empowerment

By Erica A. Moore

Get Out of Your Own Way:

A Guide to Confidence & Empowerment

Erica A. Moore

Published by:
Erica A. Moore
Bedford, 76021 TX, USA

Cover Design & Formatting: Nicole Jamison

ISBN: 979-8-218-61132-3

Printed in USA

To My Nanny,

This is for you. Thank you for always being there for all of us and for doing the best you knew how to do. I love you forever—until we meet again.

Always your little girl,

Florence R. Harden
my Great Grandmother

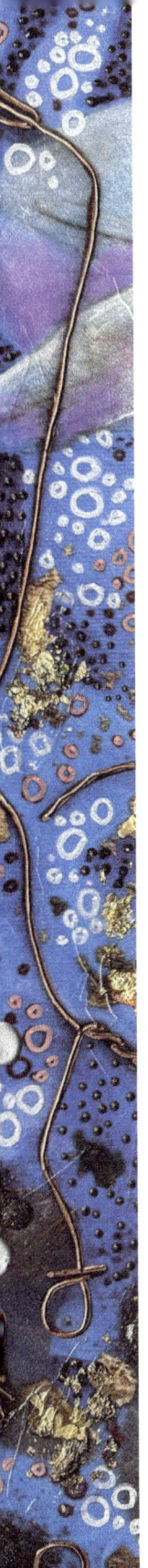

Contents

Introduction

Life can often feel like a battle between who we are and who we want to become. Depression, self-doubt, and fear can hold us back from living our fullest, most confident lives. But the truth is—you are stronger than you think. You are not alone, and you have the power to rise above your circumstances. This book is a guide to help you shift your mind-set, build resilience, and step boldly into your purpose. Each chapter includes wisdom from scripture, practical steps, and journaling prompts to help you take action. You are on a journey to becoming the best version of yourself.

Now lets get started

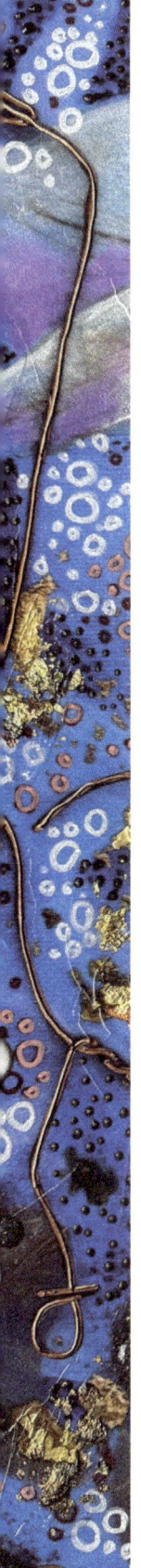

Understanding Depression & Confidence

"Psalm 34:17" - 'The righteous cry out, and the Lord hears them; he delivers them from all their troubles.'

Depression and lack of confidence can feel like a heavy weight, making even the smallest tasks seem overwhelming. But the first step to healing is recognizing that you are not alone. God hears your cries, and He is ready to guide you through your struggles.

— Practical Steps:

1. Acknowledge Your Feelings — It's okay to not be okay. Give yourself permission to feel what you feel.

2. Talk to Someone — Whether it's a trusted friend, family member, or therapist, speaking about your emotions can bring relief.

3. Start Small — Confidence grows when you take small steps forward. Set one small goal today and commit to it.

Breaking FREE from Self-Doubt

"Psalm 27:1" - 'The Lord is my light and my salvation—whom shall I fear?'

Self-doubt is often the result of past failures or fears of the unknown. It whispers lies that you are not good enough, not smart enough, not strong enough. But here's the truth: You are equipped with everything you need to succeed. God's light shines on you, giving you clarity and courage.

— Practical Steps:

1. Identify the Lies — Write down the things you doubt about yourself.

2. Replace Them with Truths — Next to each doubt, write an empowering truth about yourself.

3. Take Action Despite Fear — Confidence isn't about having no fear; it's about moving forward anyway.

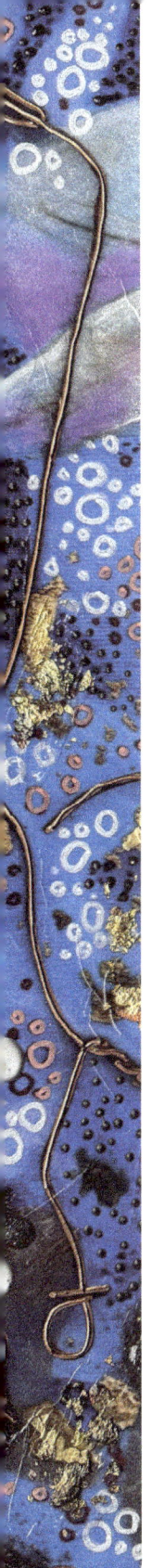

The Power of Positive Affirmations

"Psalm 46:5" – 'God is within her, she will not fall: God will help her at break of day.'

Self-doubt is often the result of past failures or fears of the unknown. It whispers lies that you are not good enough, not smart enough, not strong enough. But here's the truth: You are equipped with everything you need to succeed. God's light shines on you, giving you clarity and courage.

— Practical Steps:

1. Identify the Lies — Write down the things you doubt about yourself.

2. Replace Them with Truths — Next to each doubt, write an empowering truth about yourself.

3. Take Action Despite Fear — Confidence isn't about having no fear; it's about moving forward anyway.

Faith & Resilience

"Psalm 37:5" - 'Commit your way to the Lord; trust in him and he will do this.'

Resilience is not about avoiding failure but about rising after every setback. Faith allows you to trust that every obstacle has a purpose. Hard times don't mean you are failing; they mean you are growing.

— Practical Steps:

1. Lean on Your Faith — Pray or meditate on scripture when you feel discouraged.

2. Re-frame Setbacks — Instead of seeing failure, ask, "What is this teaching me?"

3. Keep Moving Forward — Even slow progress is progress. Take one small action every day.

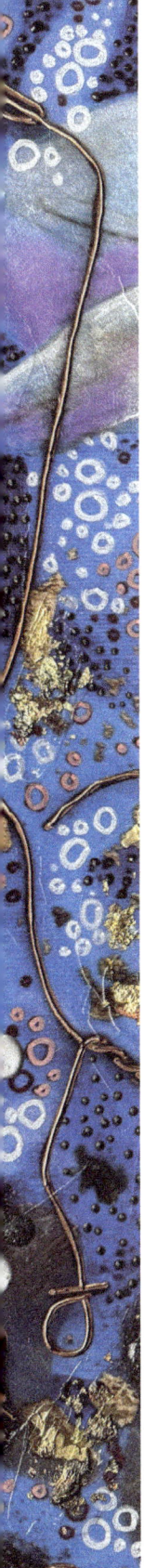

Overcoming Negative Thoughts

"Psalm 55:22" – 'Cast your cares on the Lord and he will sustain you.'

Negative thoughts will always appear, but they don't have to control you. The key is learning to manage them so they don't dictate your decisions or self-worth.

— Practical Steps:

1. Recognize the Thought — When a negative thought arises, pause and ask, "Is this true?"

2. Challenge It — If it's not true, replace it with a more empowering belief.

3. Practice Gratitude — Shifting focus to what you're grateful for helps reframe negative thoughts.

Keep Going

A JOURNALING GUIDE

Journaling is a powerful tool for self-discovery and emotional healing. These pages will guide you through reflection and help you continue your journey toward confidence and joy.

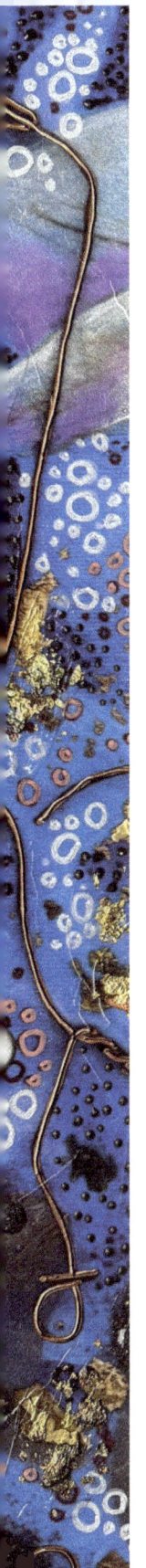

KEEP GOING

"Psalm 118:24" – 'This is the day the Lord has made; let us rejoice and be glad in it.'
Every day is a new opportunity to grow and heal. Write about one thing you're looking forward to today, no matter how small.

KEEP GOING

"Psalm 30:5" – 'Weeping may stay for the night, but rejoicing comes in the morning.'

Tough times don't last forever. What is one difficulty you've faced that eventually led to something good?

_____

_____

_____

_____

_____

_____

_____

_____

_____

_____

_____

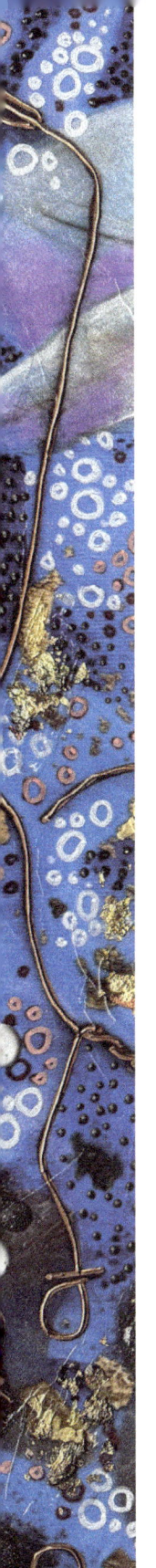

KEEP GOING

"Psalm 121:1–2" – 'I lift up my eyes to the mountains—where does my help come from? My help comes from the Lord.'

Where do you find your strength? Reflect on a time when you felt supported or uplifted.

KEEP GOING

"Psalm 23:4" – 'Even though I walk through the darkest valley, I will fear no evil, for you are with me.'

Fear is natural, but faith can help you push past it. What is something you fear that you want to conquer?

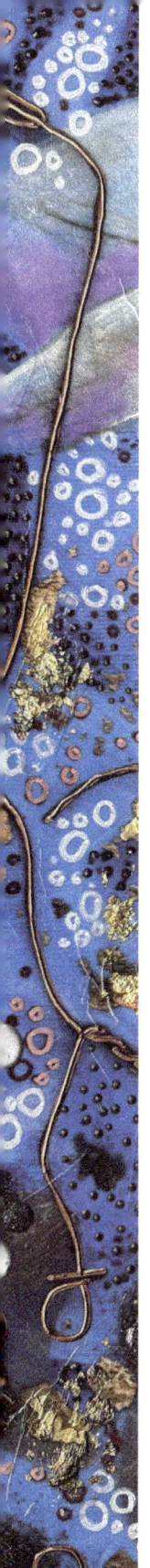

KEEP GOING

"Psalm 139:14" – 'I praise you because I am fearfully and wonderfully made.'

Write about one thing you love about yourself and why it makes you unique.

_____

_____

_____

_____

_____

_____

_____

_____

_____

_____

KEEP GOING

"Psalm 118:24" – 'This is the day the Lord has made; let us rejoice and be glad in it.'

Every day is a new opportunity to grow and heal. Write about one thing you're looking forward to today, no matter how small.

KEEP GOING

"Psalm 30:5" – 'Weeping may stay for the night, but rejoicing comes in the morning.'

Tough times don't last forever. What is one difficulty you've faced that eventually led to something good?

14

KEEP GOING

"Psalm 121:1–2" – 'I lift up my eyes to the mountains—where does my help come from? My help comes from the Lord.'

Where do you find your strength? Reflect on a time when you felt supported or uplifted.

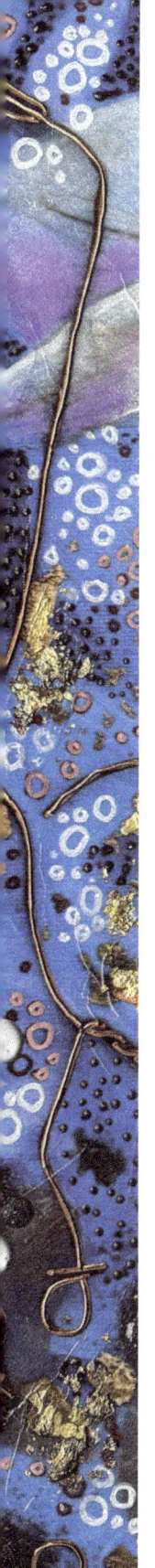

KEEP GOING

"Psalm 23:4" – 'Even though I walk through the darkest valley, I will fear no evil, for you are with me.'

Fear is natural, but faith can help you push past it. What is something you fear that you want to conquer?

KEEP GOING
"Psalm 139:14" – 'I praise you because I am fearfully and wonderfully made.'

Write about one thing you love about yourself and why it makes you unique.

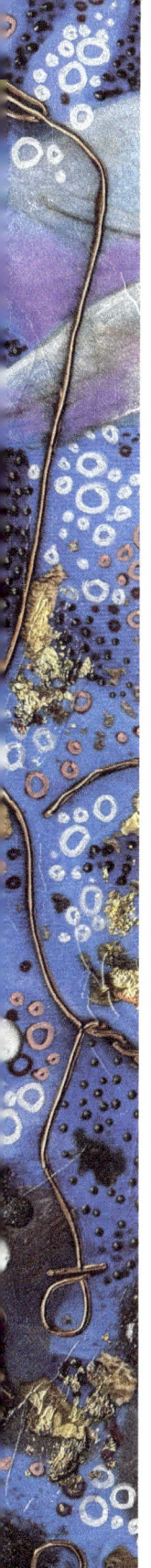

KEEP GOING

"Psalm 118:24" – 'This is the day the Lord has made; let us rejoice and be glad in it.'

Every day is a new opportunity to grow and heal. Write about one thing you're looking forward to today, no matter how small.

KEEP GOING

"Psalm 30:5" – 'Weeping may stay for the night, but rejoicing comes in the morning.'

Tough times don't last forever. What is one difficulty you've faced that eventually led to something good?

_____

_____

_____

_____

_____

_____

_____

_____

_____

_____

_____

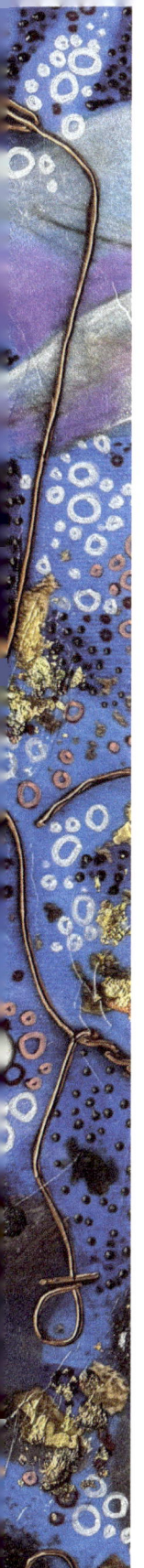

KEEP GOING

"Psalm 121:1-2" – 'I lift up my eyes to the mountains—where does my help come from? My help comes from the Lord.'

Where do you find your strength? Reflect on a time when you felt supported or uplifted.

KEEP GOING

"Psalm 23:4" – 'Even though I walk through the darkest valley, I will fear no evil, for you are with me.'

Fear is natural, but faith can help you push past it. What is something you fear that you want to conquer?

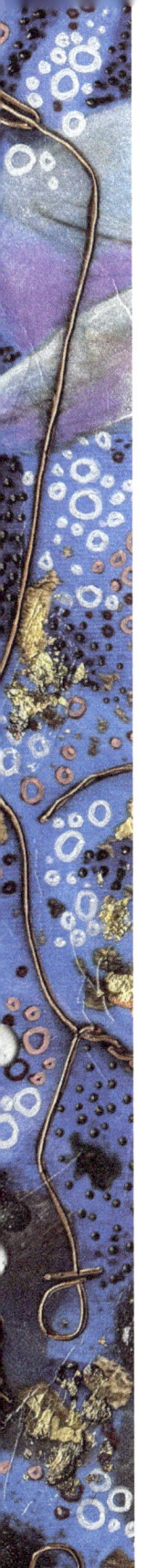

KEEP GOING

"Psalm 139:14" – 'I praise you because I am fearfully and wonderfully made.'

Write about one thing you love about yourself and why it makes you unique.

22

KEEP GOING

"Psalm 118:24" – 'This is the day the Lord has made; let us rejoice and be glad in it.'

Every day is a new opportunity to grow and heal. Write about one thing you're looking forward to today, no matter how small.

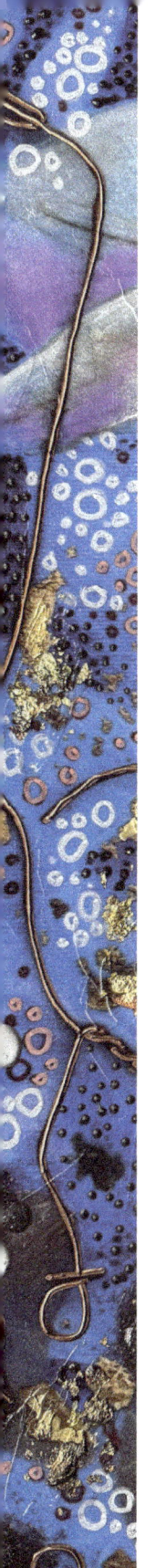

KEEP GOING

"Psalm 30:5" – 'Weeping may stay for the night, but rejoicing comes in the morning.'

Tough times don't last forever. What is one difficulty you've faced that eventually led to something good?

24

KEEP GOING

"Psalm 121:1–2" – 'I lift up my eyes to the mountains—where does my help come from? My help comes from the Lord.'

Where do you find your strength? Reflect on a time when you felt supported or uplifted.

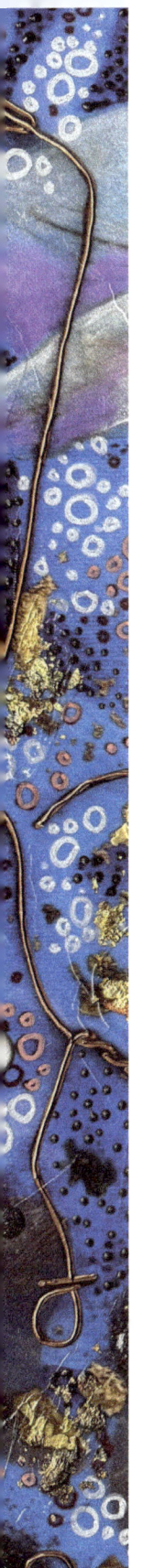

KEEP GOING

"Psalm 23:4" – 'Even though I walk through the darkest valley, I will fear no evil, for you are with me.'

Fear is natural, but faith can help you push past it. What is something you fear that you want to conquer?

KEEP GOING

"Psalm 139:14" – 'I praise you because I am fearfully and wonderfully made.'

Write about one thing you love about yourself and why it makes you unique.